FIGHT GIRL BATTLE WORLD

Qui Nguyen

BROADWAY PLAY PUBLISHING INC
224 E 62nd St, NY, NY 10065
www.broadwayplaypub.com
info@broadwayplaypub.com

FIGHT GIRL BATTLE WORLD
© Copyright 2008 by Qui Nguyen

First printing: Aug 2008, second printing: Nov 2009
I S B N: 978-0-88145-396-6

Book design: Marie Donovan
Word processing: Microsoft Word
Typographic controls: Ventura Publisher
Typeface: Palatino
Printed and bound in the U S A

FIGHT GIRL BATTLE WORLD was first produced by
Vampire Cowboys Theatre Company (Abby Marcus,
Producer). The cast and creative contributors were:

MIKAH MONOCH .... Elena Chang
ADON-RA .... Noshir Dalal
PRESIDENT YA-WI, GREE-GREE .... Jon Hoche
HURT, ZIMLEK, ANCHOR,
    ZOO-KEEPER .... Kelly Rae O'Donnell
E-V .... Melissa Paladino
J'AN JAH .... Maureen Sebastian
ZIMLEK, COMMANDER G'BRIL .... Andrea Marie Smith
BURNOUT, LC-4 .... Paco Tolson
GENERAL DAN'H .... Temar Underwood

Director .... Robert Ross Parker
Costume design .... Jessica Wegener
Scenic & lighting design .... Nick Francone
Sound design .... Patrick Shearer
Puppet design .... David Valentine
Fight direction .... Qui Nguyen
Video design .... Robert Ross Parker
Assistant stage managers .... Emily Edwards, Lex
      Friedman, Sharon Walsh, Stephanie Cox-Williams
Press Representative .... Jim Baldassare

CHARACTERS

E-V
ADON-RA
GENERAL DAN'H
J'AN JAH
LC-4
PRESIDENT YA-WI
COMMANDER G'BRIL
MIKAH MONOCH
ZOO-KEEPER
ZIMLEK
GREE-GREE
HURT
BURNOUT
R,P9ED TWO
LEADER ONE
ANCHOR
ANNOUNCER
SECRETARY
GARY THE TINGARIAN
CHINDOR THE AKITOMI

ACT ONE

PROLOGUE

(Fade in...Battle World)

(Lights come up on the silhouette of E-V, *a young, but tough looking street girl. She is in the process of taping up her hands for a fight. She sits at the corner of a make-shift ring. Her face is covered to hide her identity.)*

(Cut to...)

(In the hull of a dark warship)

J'AN JAH: The alliance patrols are not detecting us, General. It looks like the new cloaking system we picked up from Jingalo is working. We should be clear to make descent without incident.

GENERAL DAN'H: We've never traveled this far outside of the core planets, J'an. You're sure there's a human on this lizard infested rock?

J'AN JAH: The planet scan does indicate the presence of a sapian.

GENERAL DAN'H: Those scans have also sent us on more than a few wild gimda chases in the past.

J'AN JAH: Unless this is a Smordak Shapeshifter, General, the cold read definitely finds the genetic imprints of a higher functioning mammal of primate origin planetside. A female. Roughly nineteen to twenty years in age.

(Cut to...)

ANNOUNCER: In this corner weighing 51.2 kilofraks, the angry, the unstoppable, the undefeated champion of the Battle World slums, E-V the Smordak!

(Unamused, E-V waves to the crowd. They cheer.)

ANNOUNCER: And her challenger, weighing 551.2 kilofraks, CHINDOR THE AKITOMIIIIII!!!

(A much larger fighter steps onto stage. It is acted out by a gigantic puppet.)

(Focus shift to...)

J'AN JAH: Do you wish to continue our descent, General?

GENERAL DAN'H: I've spent so long hunting down and destroying their kind, J'an. If this female is indeed the last, I should be the one who finishes this.

J'AN JAH: If she does end up being a human, attempting to face her alone could prove to be fatal. Their kind are extremely dangerous.

GENERAL DAN'H: I've faced the worst kinds of horrors known to war. I'm sure one little human girl isn't going to scare me so easily.

(Cut to...)

ANNOUNCER: THIS. IS. BATTLE WORLD!!!!

(A bell rings. E-V goes at it with the fighter. She takes him out.)

(Cut to...)

J'AN JAH: What is your order?

GENERAL DAN'H: Land the ship, J'an. I'd like to meet this girl.

(Projection: Fight Girl Battle World)

Scene One

(Shift to...)

ANCHOR: *(V O)* Earlier today, the bodies of one hundred and twenty-nine Fornaxians were found brutally slain on the western outpost of the farming planet Fornax 12. Security cams were able to capture some of the violent footage from today's slaughter. We must warn you, the material you're about to see, though fuzzy, is quite graphic in nature.

(Movement sequence: lights come up on the silhouette of ADON-RA. *The stage begins to fill with the shadows of other creatures. The shadows attack.* ADON-RA *begins systematically slaying his attackers. All the shadows become one formless mass. From here, we see the shadows of torn off limbs and body parts thrown out of the dark clump.)*

*(*ADON-RA *slays all his enemies.)*

(Cut to...)

*(*ZIMLEK, *a two headed lizard alien, enters* E-V's *locker room. He is dressed like a 1920s gangster. A radio plays in the background.)*

ANCHOR: *(V O)* It is believed that this mass killing is connected to a series of attacks being committed by Adon-Ra, the leader of the Outer World insurgents that's claimed over twelve thousand victims including the very tragic events at Klobal.

*(*E-V *is mending her wounds.)*

ZIMLEK: What do you think of this Adon-Ra business? Scary

stuff. But you have to admire him. He's really made a name for himself.

E-V: He's a mass murderer, Zimlek. That's not exactly the kind of thing that puts you into the history-core in a positive light.

ZIMLEK: But it does put you in the history-core.

E-V: Zimlek, if you haven't noticed, I'm a little bit upset here.

ZIMLEK: Is that so?

E-V: Yeah. That so.

ZIMLEK: And what is wrong, my pet? Was it something I said?

E-V: More like something you didn't say, Zim. You didn't tell me I was fighting an Akitomi Demon.

ZIMLEK: Did I not? Hmmm, sorry. Must have slipped my mind.

E-V: I should have been warned. Those things are bad news.

ZIMLEK: Obviously not as bad as a human.

E-V: Don't call me that.

ZIMLEK: Apologies. I forget how sensitive you can be about your heritage.

E-V: Just give me my cut, Zim. I have wounds to bandage.

ZIMLEK: Not so fast, pet. I have another job for you. It's against a Tingarian Warrior from the Basilisk region.

E-V: A Tingarian? I cut my teeth bringing down those oversized bug-eaters. How do you think I got my rep in the first place?

ZIMLEK: Oh, I'm quite aware of your reputation against Tingarians. So is every other bookie on Battle World. That's why I want you to throw the match.

E-V: What?

ZIMLEK: More glory in betting for the underdog.

E-V: No way.

ZIMLEK: You've mistaken this as a request. I'm not requesting. I'm telling.

E-V: And I'm saying no.

ZIMLEK: You know, E-V, there's collectors out there who would love to have you as part of their zoo. The last human. A lot of planets would pay top dollar for an attraction like that.

E-V: Is that a threat?

ZIMLEK: It's an interesting thought.
   Remember, human girl, I was the one who saved you. If it weren't for me, you'd be burnt embers like the rest of your species.

E-V: Maybe you should have just left me there to die.

ZIMLEK: Don't say that, pet. I'd be very sad if something were to ever happen to you. You're like a daughter to me.

E-V: You don't really mean that, Zim.

ZIMLEK: Of course I do, my pet. I took care of you, didn't I? I trained you. I hid you when others would have slain you at first sight. No one cares about you like I do, E-V. No one ever will. I am your family.

(E-V *exits.*)

Scene Two

(Cut to...)

(Movement sequence: As jazz music plays, we see GENERAL DAN'H *standing on a streetside watching* E-V *leave her locker room. He follows her as she walks home.)*

(E-V enters her living quarters. It's a junky space. Dirty, old, and clearly not meant for occupants. She greets a strange creature that's her pet.)

E-V: Hello there, Boogie. You love me, don't you? You don't care that I'm a scary human. You are my very bestest...and only...friend. *(She gives her pet a kiss.)*

(In the shadows, we see GENERAL DAN'H. *He goes to grab* E-V.)

GENERAL DAN'H: Human!

(E-V immediately turns to defend herself. She kicks GENERAL DAN'H *to the ground.)*

E-V: What the durk are you doing in my living space?

(GENERAL DAN'H easily recovers. He charges at E-V *again. She grabs any item she can to hit him with. It doesn't stop him.)*

(E-V tries to run away, but GENERAL DAN'H *grabs her and tosses her through a wall.)*

E-V: Qward me, that hurts.

GENERAL DAN'H: I need you to come with me.

E-V: And I need you to sit the durk down!

(E-V kicks GENERAL DAN'H's *legs out from underneath him. He falls face first to the ground.)*

(E-V immediately takes the advantage and begins pommeling him in the head.)

E-V: Stay down, stay down, stay down—

(GENERAL DAN'H *grabs* E-V *by the throat and stands back up lifting her off the ground.*)

E-V: Okay. Or do whatever you like.

GENERAL DAN'H: You humans are so utterly bothersome.

E-V: Is that why you're gonna kill me? Cause I'm bothersome?

(GENERAL DAN'H *lowers* E-V.)

GENERAL DAN'H: I'm not here to kill you.

E-V: Well, you got a funny way of showing it.

GENERAL DAN'H: You hit me. That made me mad.

E-V: Okay. Well, jumping out of shadows doesn't exactly elicit the most gracious of responses out of me. Sorry.

GENERAL DAN'H: As am I.

E-V: Now. Can you explain to me. Calmly. What are you doing here?

GENERAL DAN'H: My name is Dan'h Madrin. I was a General for the Alliance during the Human Wars.

E-V: Dan'h Madrin?

GENERAL DAN'H: I led forces against—

E-V: You're General Dan'h Madrin?

GENERAL DAN'H: Yes. You know of me?

E-V: Of course I know who the qward you are. You're the needle-weeder who blew up my planet!

(E-V *goes to attack* GENERAL DAN'H *again.*)

(*He points a gun at her.*)

GENERAL DAN'H: I apologize for the need for
self-protection, but let my intentions speak clear,
I am not here to fight you. I am here to help you.

E-V: You? Help me? Right. Maybe you shouldn't have
executed everyone in my race. That would have been
helpful.

GENERAL DAN'H: I'm sorry for what I've done. I wish
to make amends for it.

E-V: Then just let me kill ya and we'll call it even.

GENERAL DAN'H: I know how to save your people.

E-V: There's no people left to save, durk-raker. I'm the
last human.

GENERAL DAN'H: That's where you are wrong. There is
another.

E-V: Who?

(Cut to...)

*(A shrouded figure [*HURT*] sitting at an alien cantina.)*

(We then see BURNOUT *and* ADON-RA *[who's in disguise]
drinking.)*

BURNOUT: I'm telling ya, buddy—it was a mess.
I was drowning in qwarding humans. They had me
surrounded—breathin' down my qwardin' neck like
service-droid at a bachelor party.

ADON-RA: Holy durk.

BURNOUT: You ever seen a human up close?

ADON-RA: Naw, Bro. Never.

BURNOUT: They are one ugly species. But violent.
Qwardin' eat your kids—qwardin' rape your women
without a second thought. My bro tried to befriend one
back before the human wars—you know, he was one of
those old worlder types. Thought all the rumors about

them monkeys were just talk. Ya know what happened
to him?

ADON-RA: What?

BURNOUT: His primate buddy shot him in the back of
the head and ate his face. In front of his whole family.
And then...he raped the guy's pets.

ADON-RA: Durk.

BURNOUT: Durk is right. U G C did a good thing when
they made it legal to kill humans. Kept us all safe. Let
us be able to protect our families from those cannibals.

ADON-RA: You can say that again.

HURT: Yeah.

(BURNOUT *and* ADON-RA *glare at the hooded figure.*)

BURNOUT: So they had me cornered, right? Humans all
over the place. We somehow wandered into one of their
nests. And they looked hungry.

ADON-RA: What did you do?

BURNOUT: I threw out some bovine meat. We kept some
on us for just this kinda trouble. Humans loves them
some bovine. Can't keep away from it. They just
swarm to it like a pack of growls. And while they's
was chomping down on that bovine, we begin shooting
them up like it was a carnival game.

ADON-RA: You're a hero, Bro. You're a qwardin' hero to
all of us.

BURNOUT: I was just doing whatever any good United
Galactic Citizen would do. Protecting our people.

ADON-RA: *(To the bartender)* Hey, get me a few shots for
my friend here!

BURNOUT: Come on, buddy. You don't have to do that.

ADON-RA: Naw. We're drinking to you, bro. We're drinking to a real U G C hero!

(ADON-RA *pulls a blaster on* BURNOUT.)

BURNOUT: Hey buddy, what are you doing? You can't do this. I work for the President.

ADON-RA: I know.

(ADON-RA *shoots* BURNOUT.)

(*The Hooded figure turns revealing that he's an alien.* ADON-RA *drops his disguise showing that he's...*)

HURT: Oh, god. You're...you're human!

ADON-RA: Yeah. That's right.

HURT: Oh, God. Oh God. Why are you doing this? Who are you?

ADON-RA: I'm Adon-Ra.

HURT: I'm sorry, man. I'm so sorry. Please don't hurt me. I ain't never even seen one of you people up close before.

ADON-RA: Well now you have.

(ADON-RA *rips a security badge off the dead body of* BURNOUT *leaving a very scared* HURT *behind.*)

Scene Three

(*Cut to...*)

(*Battle World streetside*)

GENERAL DAN'H: Please listen to reason.

E-V: No, I'm not coming with you.

GENERAL DAN'H: You must.

E-V: No, I mustn't. Why am I still even talking to you? You just blark-slapped me and killed the entire population of my species.

GENERAL DAN'H: Not all is lost.

E-V: Actually I'd say it is. Humanity is dead. The universe hates my kind. Now get over it, I certainly did.

GENERAL DAN'H: You can still replenish your species. This is good news.

E-V: With Adon-Ra? Are you kidding me? He's a psycho killing space terrorist.

GENERAL DAN'H: It's just a biological act. Regardless of his perceived psychotic tendencies, his reproductive system should be completely healthy. Mating with him should not be a problem at all.

E-V: Why couldn't you just have shown up to my doorstep to kill me instead?

GENERAL DAN'H: He'll make a perfect mate.

E-V: I'm not going to sleep with Adon-Ra.

GENERAL DAN'H: Actually, it's not sleep that we're after. We need you to have sexual intercourse to create another litter of humans.

E-V: Litter?

GENERAL DAN'H: Do you not breed offspring by the dozen?

E-V: I'm not a canine.

GENERAL DAN'H: I'm not inferring that you are. I'm merely inquiring, when your species lays your eggs, how many hatch?

E-V: Ya know, I hated you before for genociding my people. But now, I'm hating you for a whole different reason.

GENERAL DAN'H: For someone who wished to behead me for annihilating their species, you really don't seem too proactive in trying to make it better.

E-V: Because your solution is for me to bump uglies with an interstellar serial killer.

GENERAL DAN'H: Ooooh!

E-V: Yeah.

GENERAL DAN'H: I see. You're worried about your safety, aren't you? Worry not, E-V, I can assure you that Adon-Ra is completely safe. If you do not believe as such, we can restrain him in a full body cast with only his male reproductive organs exposed for you to copulate with. If you still don't feel comfortable with such an activity, we could also milk out his reproductive juices and insert them into you with a long tubular saturating instrument. The last thing we'd want is for you to be uncomfortable with any of this.

E-V: Um. I'm going to walk away now. Please. Don't follow me.

GENERAL DAN'H: E-V, are you really willing to let your species die out like this?

E-V: Hey, I never chose for it to get on the endangered species list in the first place, Dan'h. That was you.

GENERAL DAN'H: I'm sorry for what you have gone through. I know you may not have chosen your circumstance, but, E-V—make no mistake—in this moment, you do indeed have a choice. The future of your people's legacy is in your hands.

E-V: Who said I wanted that responsibility?

GENERAL DAN'H: Destiny isn't chosen. It's found. You can do something about this or you can just lie down and let it all end like a coward.

E-V: I'm not a coward.

GENERAL DAN'H: Then prove the universe wrong. Show them a human can do more than just kill.

(GENERAL DAN'H *hands* E-V *a transmitter.*)

E-V: What's this?

GENERAL DAN'H: In case you change your mind.

E-V: Don't follow me. I mean it.

(*As* E-V *and* GENERAL DAN'H *exit the stage,* MIKAH MONOCH *[think Boba Fett] enters the stage. It is obvious, she is tracking them.*)

(MIKAH MONOCH *flips on a wrist console that projects a face onto the back wall.*)

COMMANDER G'BRIL: What is your update?

MIKAH MONOCH: Fling tingo bong rock flu flu jong.

COMMANDER G'BRIL: What was that?

MIKAH MONOCH: Fling tingy tingy tombo.

COMMANDER G'BRIL: Say that again.

MIKAH MONOCH: Fling flangy dangy dangy ding dong.

COMMANDER G'BRIL: I'm still not understanding...you sound all weird. Maybe I should call you back on my home transmitter to see if I get a better connection.

MIKAH MONOCH: Flo flango! Apologies, Commander G'bril, I had my universal translator set to Marcopian.

COMMANDER G'BRIL: Oh, yes, I hate it when that happens. I got into the most embarrassing conversation the other day with a Blarknik who thought I was insulting the way he spoke by speaking in Yopartin. Wow, that was awkward.

MIKAH MONOCH: You were asking about my update.

COMMANDER G'BRIL: Oh yeah, how's that going?

MIKAH MONOCH: The General has landed on Il Nova
Seven—

COMMANDER G'BRIL: Battle World?

MIKAH MONOCH: Yes, sir. Battle World. And he has
made contact with a local.

COMMANDER G'BRIL: Is it Adon-Ra?

MIKAH MONOCH: No sir. This looks to be a female.

COMMANDER G'BRIL: What could he be doing that far
outside of the core?

MIKAH MONOCH: The local seems to be some sort of
street fighter. He looks to be recruiting her.

COMMANDER G'BRIL: So the General is resorting to
working with street trash now to fight the alliance.
How pathetic.

MIKAH MONOCH: What would you like me to do?

COMMANDER G'BRIL: Keep tracking him, Mikah. In
the meantime, I'm sending out a squadron of U G C
fighters to assist you in bringing him in. The president
may not think Dan'h is a threat, but we know different.
Don't we, Mikah?

MIKAH MONOCH: Hahahahaha!

(Cut to...)

Scene Four

(Lights come up on E-V *much the same way as we saw her at
the top of the play. Her face is again covered. We hear crowd
noise in anticipation of her fight. We see* ZIMLEK *in the
crowd watching.)*

ANNOUNCER: In this corner weighing 51.2 kilofraks,
the angry, the unstoppable, the undefeated champion

of the Battle World slums, E-V the Smordak!
   And her challenger, weighing 151.2 kilofraks,
GARY THE TINGARIAN!!!!

(The Tingarian warrior enters the ring.)

GARY: It will be my pleasure to finally finish you off.
Human.

E-V: What did you just call me?

GARY: Just calling you what you are.

E-V: I'm not human. I'm a Smordak.

GARY: Yeah. And I don't know what's worse. An actual
human. Or a Smordak Shapeshifter who likes to be in
the shape of one.

ANNOUNCER: THIS. IS. BATTLEWORLD!

*(The bell rings and E-V immediately lays out the Tingarian
in a single punch.)*

E-V: Qward you.

(The crowd boos. We see cups and debris get thrown at E-V.)

(Cut to...)

(Presidential chambers for PRESIDENT YA-WI)

(PRESIDENT YA-WI is played by a three-foot puppet.)

COMMANDER G'BRIL: President Ya-Wi, I beg you.
I have a location on General Dan'h. If you allot me
more resources, I'll be able to take him in.

PRESIDENT YA-WI: No.

COMMANDER G'BRIL: He's far more dangerous to us
than that single human being, Adon-Ra.

PRESIDENT YA-WI: My understanding is that I'm the
president of the United Galactic Alliance, am I not?

COMMANDER G'BRIL: Of course you are, sir.

PRESIDENT YA-WI: And you're just an officer working for the U G C.

COMMANDER G'BRIL: Sir—

PRESIDENT YA-WI: If that's the case, then why are you questioning my orders? I'm not interested in your personal vendettas, Commander. Dan'h Madrin is small-time compared to our problems with the public. What they want is the head of Adon-Ra, not the former General of the U G C. Regardless of what kind of threat Dan'h Madrin may pose, Adon-Ra is the priority. Do you understand?

COMMANDER G'BRIL: Yes, sir.

PRESIDENT YA-WI: Trust me, G'bril, once we get the human, the rest of his rebellion will fall. That includes our former General. In the meantime, the public needs assurances that our government can protect them. Give it to them.

COMMANDER G'BRIL: Yes, sir.

(Cut to...)

(In the hull of a dark warship...)

(GENERAL DAN'H storms in.)

GENERAL DAN'H: She's not coming with us!

J'AN JAH: General.

GENERAL DAN'H: Dammit. After all these years searching and fighting, we finally find a female and, low and behold, she finds the idea of mating with a human disgusting.

J'AN JAH: General Sir.

GENERAL DAN'H: Oh. My apologies, J'an. I know this is a sensitive issue for you. I didn't mean to offend. But this is just so damn—

J'AN JAH: SIR!

GENERAL DAN'H: What is it?

J'AN JAH: Two alliance fighters have just entered the
Battle World solar system. At the rate they're traveling,
they should arrive here in less than thirty milibreks.

GENERAL DAN'H: They found us? How is that possible?

J'AN JAH: I scanned the ship of all tracking detectors
and cleared the ship's GT. We should be a ghost on all
radars. There's no explanation. What would you like
me to do?

GENERAL DAN'H: If we stay here, we'll draw them
straight to E-V. DAMMIT! Prepare the engines, J'an,
it's time to leave this rock.

J'AN JAH: What about the human female?

GENERAL DAN'H: Leave her. She's obviously not the
one.

(Cut to...)

(E-V sitting in her locker room.)

(E-V pulls out the transmitter GENERAL DAN'H *has given
her and presses it. She looks up. Nothing happens.)*

E-V: Figures.

(ZIMLEK enters.)

ZIMLEK: Hello, E-V. You've been a naughty girl.

(E-V quickly stows away the device.)

E-V: I'm sorry, Zim. I owe you another fight. That
Tingarian just really pissed me off.

ZIMLEK: You're not paid to be pissed off, E-V. You're
paid to do what I say.

E-V: Look, I was having a pretty awful day, okay?
And that Tingarian called me a human.

ZIMLEK: It is what you are.

E-V: Well, I didn't get mad because he said it in an
affectionate manner, okay? It made me forget what
I was suppose to be doing up there.

ZIMLEK: You forgot? The other bookies did not forget.
I lost a lot of currency this night.

E-V: I'll earn it back.

ZIMLEK: Oh, you'll do more than just earn it back for
me, pet.

E-V: What's that suppose to mean?

ZIMLEK: I have another job lined up for you.

E-V: Zim, I can't keep fighting like this. I do have a
breaking point.

ZIMLEK: Worry not, pet. I would never want to break
you. Never. You're like kin to me afterall. I just want
the best for you.

E-V: Look, I'm really sorry, alright? Just give me a
couple nights to rest and I'll be ready to take on any
alien you want to throw at me.

ZIMLEK: Oh, you're about to see a lot of aliens where
you're going.

E-V: What are you getting at, Zim?

ZIMLEK: Your next gig is on Ticopria.

E-V: Ticopria? But that's...

ZIMLEK: A zoo planet. Correct.

(ZIMLEK *hits* E-V *with a stun gun. She falls.*)

ZIMLEK: And as it turns out—what's best for you is
even financially better for me. Pet.

Scene Five

(Cut to...)

(News report)

ANCHOR: It has been reported that Adon-Ra and his Outer World insurgents have struck again on the vacation planet of Moonbira, adding another seventy-five victims to their rampage. The heads of their victims were found severed and displayed on the beachfront spelling out the word "Guilty". The U G C is refusing to comment on this latest massacre fueling more paranoia by the citizens of United Galactic Alliance.

(Cut to...)

(A zoo. E-V wakes up inside a cell, disoriented and slightly stoned. She is dressed like a 1950s housewife.)

(In several other cells, we see other creatures.)

ZOO-KEEPER: As you can see, my little pollywogs, we've created sanctuaries that best replicate our animals' most natural environments. In this area, you can observe Jojo—

E-V: Jojo?

ZOO-KEEPER: The last human in the universe.

E-V: My name's not Jo-Jo. What am I wearing?

ZOO-KEEPER: She was found by philanthropist and animal lover, Zimlek Credok, on his homeworld of Il Nova 7.

E-V: Zimlek.

ZOO-KEEPER: Do not get too close to the glass, my little pollywogs. This is truly one of the most vicious and ferocious creatures in all of creation. There's no guarantee that our blast shield can hold up to her might.

E-V: Wow, this is really soft.

ZOO-KEEPER: Look at how she stalks about. Beware of her eyes, my little pollywogs, there's rumors that merely making eye contact with a human can be fatal. Once they hone into a victim, their lives are all but forfeit. Let us go before she decides the next life she takes is yours.

E-V: Hello! Somebody! *Help me!*

LC-4: There's no use, friend.

E-V: Who in the durk are you?

LC-4: I'm LC-4, the last survivor from the planet Lotus, the robot world.

E-V: You're a robot?

LC-4: I did just say robot *world*, didn't I? Like where the whole world is just robots? The world for robots where robots lived? Only robots?

E-V: So...

LC-4: Yes. I'm a robot.

E-V: Yeah, I knew that.

GREE-GREE: Go ga goo gee bee.

LC-4: It's alright, Gree-Gree. She seems friendly enough.

GREE-GREE: Go gibby gibby gibby.

E-V: And what's that?

LC-4: That is Gree-Gree. He's the last Greenarian.

E-V: Oh.

LC-4: And according to the tour guide, you must be Jojo.

E-V: My name isn't qwarding Jojo. It's E-V.

LC-4: Oh, yes. Those two syllables are much more pleasing to my auditory receptors than Jojo.

E-V: Was that sarcasm?

LC-4: No.

E-V: You're a robot. Robots can be sarcastic?

LC-4: Can a photon-bot calculate the Flingmar sequence in less than twenty milibreks?

E-V: Uh.

LC-4: Yes, we can be sarcastic.

E-V: Oh, good...cause that won't get old. Yeah, that's right. Two can play at that game. So how do I get out of here?

LC-4: Why would you want to do such a thing?

E-V: Because we're in a zoo.

LC-4: Oh, contrare. We're living luxuriously in a state of the art complex complete with full hospitality services including full plasma-burk infotell, G-width retrocharging, and the space-oil...Ticopria has the best space oil. What more can you ask?

E-V: This isn't a five nova hotel, robot. This is a prison.

LC-4: You can see it your way. I can see it as mine.

E-V: Hey, fuzz-butt, you know a way out of here?

GREE-GREE: Gobo dobo dobo ug nee mo.

E-V: Okay. So. No.

LC-4: The sooner you accept your lot, human friend, the happier you'll

be.

E-V: Hey, someone let me out of here!

(Cut to...)

GENERAL DAN'H: Any luck on locating that tracking device?

J'AN JAH: From this read-out, it looks to be on Ticopria.

GENERAL DAN'H: The zoo planet?

J'AN JAH: The one.

GENERAL DAN'H: Why would she be visiting there?

J'AN JAH: I don't think she's visiting, sir. Look.

GENERAL DAN'H: "Come see the newest attraction. Jojo, the last human."

J'AN JAH: General Dan'h, Ticopria is one of the most visited locations in all of the core planets. It'll be swarming with Alliance fighters. An attempted rescue could do more harm than good to both the human and ourselves if we get caught.

GENERAL DAN'H: I understand that. But I have to help her, J'an. I must.

J'AN JAH: Yes, sir.

(MIKAH MONOCH *appears on a screen in a small ship.*)

MIKAH MONOCH: Continue super pursuit mode.

GENERAL DAN'H: J'an, you're a good man. A good soldier. But you don't have to come with me on this. I've asked so much from you as is. Please tell me if this is too much and I can drop you off the nearest sentient planet.

J'AN JAH: No, sir. I can handle this. We should help her.

GENERAL DAN'H: Good.

MIKAH MONOCH: Engaging asteroid cloaking device.

GENERAL DAN'H: Set a course.

J'AN JAH: Will do. Disengaging auto-pilot.

MIKAH MONOCH: Initiate magnetic dock.

(A loud bang happens.)

GENERAL DAN'H: What was that?

J'AN JAH: We're going through an asteroid belt.

GENERAL DAN'H: Let's hope this old ship of ours can keep it together.

MIKAH MONOCH: Boarding enemy craft.

J'AN JAH: We should be there in less than twenty macrobreks.

(Cut to...)

(The other side of the ship. We see MIKAH MONOCH *secretly boarding* GENERAL DAN'H *ship as it speeds off.)*

Scene Six

(Back on Ticopria...)

(We see E-V *trying to break out of her cell to no avail.)*

(We then see LC-4 *giggling to himself.)*

E-V: Could you help me out here?

LC-4: Yes. You should definitely keep throwing yourself against that transparent blast shield because it really seems to be effective.

E-V: Why are you even in here?

LC-4: What do you mean?

E-V: Why are you here? You're a robot. Can't they just, ya know, make more of you?

LC-4: Can't they just make more of you?

E-V: I hate to tell ya this, robot, but it takes two to tango to make more humans. It's not as simple.

LC-4: And it takes a facility of the universe's most brilliant engineers to build even the most rudimentary versions of me. I do not see your point.

E-V: I'm alive.

LC-4: And you're suggesting I'm not.

E-V: Well, yeah.

LC-4: There are over three million different species in the universe and not any two are composed of the same genetic compounds, yet no one argues against any one of their statures for being living sentient creatures. However, because robots are partially made with non-organic materials such as metal and steel, somehow you believe I'm less than alive. Why is that? Why do you insist on thinking that I'm less than you.

E-V: That's not what I mean.

LC-4: Then what are you suggesting when you say I'm not alive.

(Silence)

E-V: I'm sorry, okay.

LC-4: You're apologizing?

E-V: Yeah.

LC-4: To me? But I'm a robot.

E-V: I know that.

LC-4: You are a most fascinating creature.

E-V: Even though I'm human?

LC-4: Especially because you are human.

E-V: So what kind of robot are you?

LC-4: I'm a robot robot.

E-V: No. I mean, what kind of function did you serve? Robots do have functions, right?

LC-4: Primitive ones do. Do I look primitive?

E-V: No.

LC-4: We had jobs on Lotus just like any other sentient race.

E-V: And yours?

LC-4: Isn't it obvious? I'm a fifteenth level intellect with charm, charisma, and dashing good looks. I was a robot playwright.

(E-V *smiles.*)

LC-4: Is that a smile I detect?

E-V: No.

LC-4: I believe it is. An upwardly curl of the lips along with the simultaneous contraction of vertical facial muscles—unless my optics are deceiving me, you, human friend, were indeed engaged in a smile.

E-V: You can't prove that.

LC-4: Oh. I think I can.

E-V: Oh yeah?

LC-4: Yeah.

E-V: Come on and try.

(ZOO-KEEPER *enters holding a baton.*)

ZOO-KEEPER: Hey, what's happening in here?

LC-4: Nothing, sir. We're just conversing.

ZOO-KEEPER: Making noise is what you're doing. Hey, human, you making trouble?

E-V: Hey, durk-hole, why don't you open that door and see exactly how much trouble I can make.

ZOO-KEEPER: Aw, you're a cute little monkey, you know that?

LC-4: There's no trouble, sir. We were just having a bit of a lively debate is all.

ZOO-KEEPER: How many times do I have to say this, robot? If no one is talking to you then I don't want to see those synthetic lips of yours flapping.

(ZOO-KEEPER *begins shocking* LC-4 *with her baton.*)

E-V: Stop it! Stop it!!!!

ZOO-KEEPER: Shut up! You want some of this?

E-V: I'd love some of that.

(*The* ZOO-KEEPER *goes after* E-V. LC-4, *seeing this, runs up and attacks the* ZOO-KEEPER.)

LC-4: Leave her alone!

(LC-4 *knocks out the* ZOO-KEEPER.)

LC-4: Oh, durk. I've just assaulted an authority figure.

E-V: That's great. Grab her security card and get me out of here!

LC-4: We will be heavily punished for this.

E-V: Not if we run. Come on!

LC-4: I'm not sure what to do. I've broken the first law of robotics.

E-V: Come on, LC. Let me out. I promise to keep you safe.

LC-4: Yes. I will follow you.

(LC-4 *unlocks the gates.* E-V *and* LC-4 *run off.*)

ZOO-KEEPER: (*Into a wrist-intercom*) There's been a breech in sector four! Repeat. There's been a breech in sector four. Send out the retrieval squads for an escaped human and robot. Extremely dangerous. Use lethal force if necessary. (*She collapses.*)

(*Cut to...*)

(Movement sequence: To music like The Kink's Dandy, *we see* E-V *and* LC-4 *being chased in slo-motion by Ticoprian guards. They look like they will be caught at any moment, but suddenly* GENERAL DAN'H *and his ship swoops in and takes out the troops as* E-V *and* LC-4 *jump onto his craft. They fly away.)*

Scene Seven

(Cut to...)

*(*PRESIDENT YA-WI *enters his office. He sees* ADON-RA *sitting at his desk and tries to sneak back out.)*

*(*ADON-RA *points a gun at him.)*

ADON-RA: Not so fast there, Prez.

PRESIDENT YA-WI: How did you get in here?

ADON-RA: Does that even matter? I mean, I could go into the long explanation, but it'd be merely expository. If I were you, I'd be much more concerned with the quantum blaster being pointed at your head at this moment.

PRESIDENT YA-WI: Are you going to kill me?

ADON-RA: Well. Yeah. That's why I bothered sneaking in here in the first place. Any last words?

PRESIDENT YA-WI: If you fire that weapon, you will have every soldier in the capitol swarming to this one location.

ADON-RA: Good last words.

PRESIDENT YA-WI: I know your species are famous for your ability to do violence, Adon-Ra, but even a human like yourself cannot hope to single-handedly defeat an entire planet full of military soldiers. Or am I wrong?

ADON-RA: Fine. Then I guess I'm just gonna have to punch you to death instead. That'll be equally as fun.

PRESIDENT YA-WI: If you attempt to kill me, I will have no choice but to order the execution of you and the rest of your team. Trust me, G'Bril has wanted to finish them off for years now.

ADON-RA: You know what, Ya-Wi. You're right. I don't want to shoot you. I want to draw this out. Make it a thing. You destroyed my entire species...that deserves something way more painful than just a simple shot to the head. You deserve to feel anguish in ways that the devil himself can't even imagine.

PRESIDENT YA-WI: I'm not afraid to die. If you strike me down now, I'll just come back twice as power—

(ADON-RA *shoots* PRESIDENT YA-WI.)

ADON-RA: Yeah? Well then let me see you do it.

(*An alarm starts going off.*)

ADON-RA: Aw crap.

(*Cut to...*)

(*In the hull of a dark warship*)

GENERAL DAN'H: Well, this is my warship. Along with being a fully operational and armed fighter craft, it's also equipped with—

E-V: Buttons. I get it.

GENERAL DAN'H: Are you okay?

E-V: Yeah. Thanks for saving me and the tin-can here. Not alotta folks woulda done that.

GENERAL DAN'H: Save your thanks for later until after I finish saving you and your people.

E-V: So now what?

GENERAL DAN'H: We bring you to a safe haven planet where you'll be hidden from the U G C until my pilot and I can make contact with Adon-Ra.

E-V: You can just call up Adon-Ra? What? He's on your speed-dial or something.

GENERAL DAN'H: We do have our ways.

LC-4: Human friend E-V, this ship doesn't seem very safe. Its computer is archaic and it looks to be completely void of any sort of AI.

GENERAL DAN'H: I assure you, you are completely safe here on my vessel.

J'AN JAH: The boosters are burning at full, General. We should be approaching the Beta Junction Wormhole in less than five.

GENERAL DAN'H: Good.

E-V: Holy durk. Look at you!

GENERAL DAN'H: This is my pilot, J'an Jah.

J'AN JAH: Please. Refrain from touching me.

E-V: You're human!

J'AN JAH: Actually, I'm a pilot.

E-V: I'm not talking about your job, stupid. I'm talking about what you are. Where you're from.

J'AN JAH: I'm from Ursa Minor.

E-V: Ursa what?

J'AN JAH: We're known for our extensive library and our fine intergalactic cartography.

LC-4: Map-making.

E-V: But you're human, right?

J'AN JAH: Negative. I'm an Ursalean.

E-V: But you look just like me.

LC-4: There is one small difference.

J'AN JAH: I'm the male of my species. And you're wrong, robot. It's not small. Now if you don't mind, I have a ship to fly. She's never left planetside, has she?

GENERAL DAN'H: Not once.

J'AN JAH: Explains why she's such an artard.

E-V: Wow. She's a real...sweetie.

J'AN JAH: I try. Now sit back, human girl. And prepare for hyper space. In five, four, three, two...

(J'AN JAH *hits the hyperspeed button and the ship rockets forward. Music like* California Love *by Tupac begins playing in the background as our team bob their heads to it.)*

(As the music continues, MIKAH MONOCH *makes her presence known on* GENERAL DAN'H's *ship.)*

E-V: Holy durk, where did she come from?

MIKAH MONOCH: How ya doin' there, Dan'h? Long time, no see.

GENERAL DAN'H: Mikah Monoch, how did I know G'bril would end up sending you after me.

E-V: You know her? He knows her?

J'AN JAH: Shut it or you'll get us killed.

GENERAL DAN'H: This is my former pilot, Mikah Monoch.

MIKAH MONOCH: Stress on the word "former". I see you're resorting to recruiting androids and—

E-V: I'm an Ursalean. Just like her. Him. Maps?

MIKAH MONOCH: Ursaleans to follow you. I suppose they are the only lifeforms foolish enough to listen to your commands.

LC-4: Incorrect, my intelligence circuitry is far beyond that of any known organic lifeforms. I'm able to—

(MIKAH MONOCH *hits* LC-4 *in the face.*)

(LC-4 *falls.*)

MIKAH MONOCH: Just like a robot. They can talk to any computer in the universe, but still can't take a punch.

J'AN JAH: Wow, you're really tough.

MIKAH MONOCH: J'an! And how are you, love? Still not able to work a jetpack properly?

J'AN JAH: My aerial skills have vastly improved since our days in the academy.

MIKAH MONOCH: Is that right?

J'AN JAH: It would be my pleasure to show you exactly how good I've gotten.

MIKAH MONOCH: Yeah, I'm sure you would, blark.

GENERAL DAN'H: If you a lay a hand on him—

MIKAH MONOCH: Your pilot isn't who you should be worried for, Dan'h. It's you, General. You have been a very naughty boy. And you know what happens to naughty boys, Dan'h. They get spanked. (*She activates her transmitter.*) Commander G'bril. I have some news for you.

COMMANDER G'BRIL: So, Mikah, what do you have to report?

MIKAH MONOCH: I've taken Dan'h's ship and his crew.

COMMANDER G'BRIL: That's good, Mikah. That's very good. Why hello there, General Dan'h! You look worse for the wears.

GENERAL DAN'H: G'bril, you treacherous little hamster.

COMMANDER G'BRIL: You've given the alliance quite some trouble.

GENERAL DAN'H: Qward you!

COMMANDER G'BRIL: General, it'll be good to see you again face to face. I've missed interacting with you. We have tons to talk about. Mikah, execute the lot of them and bring the General to me.

MIKAH MONOCH: Yes, Commander. It will be my pleasure.

(COMMANDER G'BRIL's screen shuts off.)

MIKAH MONOCH: Sorry, ladies, you heard the order.

(MIKAH MONOCH preps to shoot J'AN JAH, but the crew attacks her.)

J'AN JAH: So who's the blark now?

(An explosion!)

E-V: What in the qward was that?

J'AN JAH: We're getting fired upon!

(MIKAH MONOCH runs away.)

LC-4: Alert. Mikah is getting away!

GENERAL DAN'H: Don't worry about her, LC-4, we have bigger troubles coming at us.

J'AN JAH: We have two Alliance Fighters trailing us.

LC-4: Z-class Starfighters.

(Cut to...)

(The cockpits of two masked enemy fighters.)

LEADER ONE: Are you okay, sir? We saw your alert.

(A screen appears showing MIKAH MONOCH running thru GENERAL DAN'H's ship.)

MIKAH MONOCH: Dan'h's crew is stronger than they look. His new Ursalean recruit fights like a human.

LEADER ONE: Perhaps it is a human, sir.

MIKAH MONOCH: Right, like Dan'h would ever work with a...wait just a minute, that Ursalean is a human!

LEADER ONE: Human! Did you just say human? I hate humans!

RED TWO: Yeah, I'm not too fond of them either.

LEADER ONE: What's your order, sir? Red Two and I are both locked on. We have clear shots to bring them down.

MIKAH MONOCH: Shoot them down!

(*Explosion!*)

MIKAH MONOCH: But wait until I get off the ship first, please.

LEADER ONE: Sorry.

RED TWO: Sorry.

(*Cut to...*)

J'AN JAH: There's no way we can out maneuver them at this speed.

GENERAL DAN'H: How's the ship?

J'AN JAH: Our blast shields are still holding. But another hit like that—

GENERAL DAN'H: How far are we from the nearest wormhole?

J'AN JAH: At full, we can get to the Alpha Blue tunnel in seven millibreks.

GENERAL DAN'H: You'll have those seven millibreks, J'an. Just keep us moving and I'll get rid of those starfighters. LC-4, do you know how to shoot a photon cannon?

LC-4: I once wrote a play about interstellar dog-fights. It was called *All My Suns*.

GENERAL DAN'H: I'll take that as a yes.

E-V: What are you going to do?

GENERAL DAN'H: We're taking the auxiliary fighter out and shooting those goons down.

J'AN JAH: You'll have to re-dock in five for me to be able to make the leap.

GENERAL DAN'H: Understood. If we don't make it—

J'AN JAH: You will.

GENERAL DAN'H: But if we don't—

J'AN JAH: And I'm saying you will.

GENERAL DAN'H: Just make sure E-V completes her mission.

(Cut to...)

MIKAH MONOCH: Leader One and Red Two, I'm now clear of the ship. Feel free to blast them out of the sky whenever you like.

LEADER ONE & RED TWO: Yes, sir!

MIKAH MONOCH: It's a pity. They never even had a chance. *(She flies off.)*

LEADER ONE: You heard'em, Red Two. Let's show these Alliance traitors what we think of 'em. Yee-haw!

(Cut to...)

(Spaceship fight sequence using spaceship puppets)

J'AN JAH: Opening exterior hatch, General, in five. Four. Three. Two.

E-V: Be careful out there, LC-4.

LC-4: We will, human friend E-V.

GENERAL DAN'H: As soon as I engage my thrusters, J'an. I want you two to hit the engines at full. Do you understand?

J'AN JAH: Yes, sir.

GENERAL DAN'H: Peace to you all.

J'AN JAH: And to you.

GENERAL DAN'H: Let's go, robot. Engaging rear boosters.

(Cut to...)

*(*LEADER ONE *and* RED TWO*)*

LEADER ONE: Hey! Where'd they go?

RED TWO: That ship is faster than it looks.

LEADER ONE: Do a scan, Red Two. See if we can't get them back on radar.

RED TWO: Leader one, I'm detecting a second fighter.

LEADER ONE: What?

RED TWO: A second enemy fighter.

LEADER ONE: Oh. That's not good.

RED TWO: Yeah. Tell me about it. I wasn't even suppose to be come to work today.

(Music like Kenny Loggin's Danger Zone *begins playing as* GENERAL DAN'H's *craft takes focus again.)*

GENERAL DAN'H: Any signs of them, LC-4?

LC-4: There's something on the radar. It's coming in quick.

GENERAL DAN'H: Where are they?

LC-4: Oh no! They're right behind us!

LEADER ONE: Attack! Attack!

RED TWO: Okay, okay, you don't have to yell at me.

LEADER ONE: Watch out, Red Two!

(The ships seperate, preparing for their second swipe.)

LEADER ONE: Oh, they're good. This should be fun.

RED TWO: Fun? You wanna know what's fun? How about actually having my day off? That'd be fun.

LC-4: Um, General Dan'h? Please inform me you have a plan here.

GENERAL DAN'H: Oh yeah, I'm gonna do some fancy flying.

LC-4: That's not much of a plan.

LEADER ONE: Let's get'em, Red!

(They attack.)

(RED TWO gets hit.)

RED TWO: Dammit, they hit me!

LEADER ONE: Hang on tight, Red. I got your back!

LC-4: General, missiles are coming in from the left side.

(LEADER ONE hits GENERAL DAN'H's ship!)

LC-4: They struck our boosters, General! We're losing speed.

GENERAL DAN'H: I see that, robot. Calm down.

LC-4: Sorry. I'm not used to being shot at!

LEADER ONE: Now look at who's in trouble. What's up, ya qwarding needle-weeders! Wanna phone home?

RED TWO: Seriously, Leader One. Is all this taunting necessary? It does leave us pretty vulnerable.

GENERAL DAN'H: Fire side lasers now!

(GENERAL DAN'H *hits both the enemy ships.*)

LEADER ONE: Dammit!

RED TWO: Yeah. I totally saw that coming.

(*They reset to soar past one another.*)

LEADER ONE: Okay, Red Two. Enough playing around. Let's run these durkholes down!

RED TWO: We're were playing?

LC-4: Evade! Evade!

GENERAL DAN'H: I'm trying!

(*The ships sweep at each other,* GENERAL DAN'H *evades making the two enemy ships collide.*)

RED TWO: I think I got a shot! I'm going in!

LEADER ONE: No, Red! You're flying too close to them!

GENERAL DAN'H: I have you now!

RED TWO: Oh, man, and I wasn't even suppose to be here today. *Aaaahhh!*

(RED TWO *is shot down.*)

LEADER ONE: *Red!*

(LEADER ONE *jumps onto the puppeteer playing* GENERAL DAN'H's *ship.*)

LC-4: They're on our rear! They're on our rear!

GENERAL DAN'H: I'm trying to shake them off, LC-4. They're on us too tight.

LEADER ONE: Let's see what happens when I do this!

(LEADER ONE *puppeteer bites* GENERAL DAN'H's *puppeteer.*)

GENERAL DAN'H: Aaaah!

LC-4: Aaaah!

(GENERAL DAN'H *shakes off the fighter.*)

GENERAL DAN'H: What in the qward was that?

LC-4: I think they just bit us.

GENERAL DAN'H: Now it's time to get on the offensive. You with me, robot?

LC-4: I don't think I have a choice.

LEADER ONE: Oh, you wanna go nose to nose? Let's go nose to nose.

GENERAL DAN'H: Aaaaah!

LC-4: Aaaaah!

LEADER ONE: Aaaaah!

(*The culmination of the fight has both fighters speeding nose to nose to one another with* GENERAL DAN'H, LC-4, *and* LEADER ONE *screaming.*)

(*Cut to...*)

(*Quiet*)

(*In the hull of a dark warship*)

J'AN JAH: General Dan'h. General Dan'h, do you read me? Buckle up, human. We're about to hit the Alpha Blue Wormhole in...Five. Four. Three. Two.

Scene Nine

(*The President's chamber*)

(*We see* PRESIDENT YA-WI *breath his last couple of breaths before his passes out behind his desk.*)

(*We then begin hearing and seeing the glow of some sort of transformation happening behind the desk.*)

(Suddenly, PRESIDENT YA-WI's *hand reaches onto the desk. Then we see his hood. He stands up fully erect and we discover he is now no longer a small creature, but of human size. He examines himself. We do not see his face.)*

PRESIDENT YA-WI: This is most...interesting. *(He calmly walks to his desk and presses his intercom.)* Get me G'bril on the line. Tell her to bring those rebel scum to me.

SECRETARY: Who is this?

PRESIDENT YA-WI: This is your president speaking.

Scene Ten

(The hull of a dark warship. J'AN JAH *is working on the ship.)*

E-V: We should go back.

J'AN JAH: I'm trying to work here, human.

E-V: Seriously, J'an. They could use our help. We have a big ship. We should be able to do something, right?

J'AN JAH: I am trying to do something. I'm trying to fix our stabilizers.

E-V: The ship feels fine. It feels stable.

J'AN JAH: That's not what stabilizers do.

E-V: Then who cares?

J'AN JAH: Do you know what happens when you try to land a ship without stabilizers?

E-V: No.

J'AN JAH: You crash, human. You crash.

E-V: I have a name, J'an, and it's not "human".

J'AN JAH: I'm just calling you by what you are.

E-V: And what if I just called you by "what you are"?

J'AN JAH: I'm proud of my heritage, thank you.

E-V: Oh, so you're proud of being from a long lineage of space bitch?

J'AN JAH: Need I remind you that I am the male of my species. *(She removes her helmet showing that she is a very attractive female actress.)*

E-V: Obviously. Still doesn't make you any less of a bitch though, now does it?

(J'AN JAH raises her fist...and then smacks the control panel. The ship's systems turn back on.)

J'AN JAH: But it does make me one amazing mechanic.

(Cut to...)

(The cockpit of GENERAL DAN'H and LC-4's starfighter. GENERAL DAN'H is unconscious.)

LC-4: General Dan'h. General Dan'h. General Dan'h. General Dan'h.

GENERAL DAN'H: What in the blazes? Am I dead?

LC-4: Um, yes. You're dead. You're in heaven. This is heaven. Ooooooh heaven. Isn't this great? Looks a liiiittle like a cockpit, but at least we're together.

GENERAL DAN'H: Enough, LC-4. Where are we?

LC-4: We are currently free floating in the middle the Dancorprium region of outer space.

GENERAL DAN'H: What's our status?

LC-4: Our boosters have been destroyed. We have no propulsion. Luckily, the self-sustaining atmosphere controls are intact allowing you to maintain consciousness. The oxygen battery still has enough power to keep you alive for another twenty-two macrobreks.

(The dead body of RED TWO *floats by and slams into the ship.)*

GENERAL DAN'H: Oh God! What was that?

LC-4: That would be the lifeless body of the enemy pilot.

GENERAL DAN'H: We have to get this craft moving again, LC-4, or we're going to be no better than that floating carcass out there.

LC-4: Agreed.

GENERAL DAN'H: So, robo-brain. Got any ideas?

LC-4: We are currently floating 51.4 macroliks from the wreckage of the enemy ship. From this vantage point, it looks like his booster system is still intact. If we can retrofit his booster to our craft, we will be able to achieve forward progression.

GENERAL DAN'H: You're talking spacewalk, robot?

LC-4: Indeed.

GENERAL DAN'H: And how are we suppose to pull that off?

LC-4: I thought I could tie a rope to you and use your body as a fishing hook to grab it.

GENERAL DAN'H: What?

LC-4: I am joking. Unlike yourself, my body does not require oxygen. I could be able to do the walk just fine.

GENERAL DAN'H: But without something anchoring you, there's a good chance you'll be swept into deep space.

LC-4: A sixty-seven-point-eight percent chance.

GENERAL DAN'H: That's a big risk.

LC-4: No durk, durklock. If there was a better option, don't you think I would have suggested that first?

GENERAL DAN'H: Okay, okay, I understand.

LC-4: It is our best option.

GENERAL DAN'H: Is there anything I can do?

LC-4: Pray.

(Cut to...)

(E-V and J'AN JAH)

J'AN JAH: Get out of my way, E-V.

E-V: Are you going to fly us back?

J'AN JAH: No.

E-V: Then I'm not moving.

J'AN JAH: Don't be—

E-V: What? Stupid? Violent? Ugly? What else are you going to throw at me here, Urgo?

J'AN JAH: Urgo?

E-V: It's my new derogatory term for Ursaleans. How does that make you feel, Urgo?

J'AN JAH: Stop that. You're acting like a—

E-V: Like what? An Urgo?

J'AN JAH: A child.

E-V: I want to go back.

J'AN JAH: Too bad.

E-V: Then I guess we're just gonna sit here floating in space.

J'AN JAH: Fine. You wanna fly the ship? Be my guest. Do you have a pilot's license? Is that something you picked up on Battle World between prize fighting and *eating babies*?

E-V: I don't eat babies

J'AN JAH: Humans don't eat babies?

E-V: No.

J'AN JAH: Oh. Weird. Well, whether you've swallowed this fact yet or not, we are trying to help you. We're trying to give you something you've never had before. A life. A family. A chance at surviving. And we're risking our lives to do it—so get over yourself and get out of my way. Now.

(Cut to...)

GENERAL DAN'H: Are you ready, LC-4?

LC-4: No.

GENERAL DAN'H: Um...when will you be?

LC-4: General Dan'h, this is not a procedure I am ever going to be completely comfortable in performing.

GENERAL DAN'H: So does that mean you're never going to do this?

LC-4: It means...I am as ready as I'll ever be.

GENERAL DAN'H: Okay. Your cockpit hatch will be opening in five. Four. Three. Two.

(The hatch opens.)

(Music like a piece from Giacomo Puccini's Turandot *begins playing.*

(LC-4 gracefully floats out of the ship. He pushes off and free floats into outer space curiously exploring zero gravity.)

GENERAL DAN'H: How is it out there in zero gravity? That must be a pretty strange sensation. You look like you're flying.

LC-4: Yes, General, that is quite an observation.

GENERAL DAN'H: Is it scary?

LC-4: Yes.

GENERAL DAN'H: Is it weird?

LC-4: Yes.

GENERAL DAN'H: Is it fun?

LC-4: General!

GENERAL DAN'H: Sorry.

LC-4: I am now docking with the craft.

GENERAL DAN'H: Really, is there anything I can do? Cause I'm just sitting here watching you.

LC-4: No. I'm fine, General Dan'h. I'm quite capable of removing a booster rocket myself.

GENERAL DAN'H: Okay. You're looking good out there. Good job.

LC-4: Thank you.

GENERAL DAN'H: I wonder how E-V and J'an are doing.

(Cut to...)

J'AN JAH: We're here, human. The desert planet of Peña 15.

E-V: So this is what we're doing instead of saving Dan'h and LC? Wow. Great.

J'AN JAH: It's what they would have wanted.

E-V: So this is the safe haven?

J'AN JAH: Incorrect. I've brought you somewhere else.

E-V: Is this some kind of trick?

J'AN JAH: This is where we will find Adon-Ra.

E-V: Here? How can you be so sure?

J'AN JAH: Because, E-V. Adon-Ra is my husband.
   Aieeeeee!

(We hear an animal sound.)

E-V: What?

J'AN JAH: Tut-tut! Here comes our ride.

E-V: Ya gotta be kidding me.

(Cut to...)

GENERAL DAN'H: How are you doing out there, LC-4?

LC-4: That is an unnecessary inquiry.

GENERAL DAN'H: Why, robot? Because you're a vastly
intelligent mechanized being that doesn't need the help
of an organic like myself.

LC-4: No.

GENERAL DAN'H: Then what is it?

(The shadow of a large spaceship goes over GENERAL DAN'H
and LC-4.*)*

LC-4: The United Galactic Alliance has caught up with
us.

*(*COMMANDER G'BRIL *and* MIKAH MONOCH *come up on
screen.)*

G'BRIL: General Dan'h. Fancy meeting you out here.

GENERAL DAN'H: Dammit!

END OF ACT ONE

ACT TWO

(The ZOO-KEEPER *enters the stage.)*

ZOO-KEEPER: Hello, my little pollywogs, and welcome to the middle of the play. Did you know that there could still be humans among us? Oh, yes, our beloved President Ya-Wi has gone a long way in trying to eradicate this very dangerous species, but there is no guarantee that we completely wiped out this very viscous animal.

How is this possible you might ask?

Well, as infants, humans are affectionate, playful, and irresistibly cute.

(Projection: A cute baby)

ZOO-KEEPER: For this reason, some misguided Alliance citizens may be tempted to keep a surviving human toddler as a pet. But, beware, humans do not make good pets!

At an early age, Humans may seem to be harmless and fun, but humans, like any animal, grow up fast, and by puberty, they are stronger than most adult Tingarians and become very destructive, irrational, and very very dangerous.

And as we all know, adult humans are not cute or friendly.

(Projection: A really out-of-shape and scary looking adult)

ZOO-KEEPER: Adult humans can and will bite. And not only can a human harm you, but they can also harm

your children. Humans are also notorious baby eaters.
They will sneak into your nests, steal your eggs, and,
without a second thought, eat your unborn babies for
breakfast.

(Projection: A plate of scrambled eggs and bacon)

ZOO-KEEPER: So, please, if you know of anyone in
possession of a human, for their safety and the safety
of the public—report them immediately to your local
U G C agency.
    Remember, only you can prevent humanity.

Scene One

*(Lights come up on E-V and J'AN JAH on the Peña 15
planetside.)*

(They are riding some sort of Taun-Taun-like creature.)

E-V: So what do you mean Adon-Ra is your husband?

J'AN JAH: Excuse me. Once was my husband. We're
divorced.

E-V: Once was your husband? But I thought you were
male.

J'AN JAH: I am. Do you have an issue with that?

E-V: No. No. I just...does Dan'h know about this?

J'AN JAH: Of course he does. We all work together.

E-V: So that's why you've been so touchy with me
this whole time.

J'AN JAH: I have not been touchy with you.

E-V: Riiight.

J'AN JAH: What are you getting at, human?

E-V: J'an. Come on. Tell me the truth here, girl to
almost-girl...you don't want me to do this, do you?

J'AN JAH: Do what?

E-V: Mate with your husband.

J'AN JAH: Ex-husband.

E-V: Ex-husband.

(Silence)

J'AN JAH: No. I want you to do it.

E-V: You do?

J'AN JAH: It is for the good of your people and the universe.

E-V: Oh. That's really...thoughtful of you?

J'AN JAH: Ursaleans are very selfless creatures.

E-V: J'an. You don't have to—

J'AN JAH: I am done talking about this subject, E-V. What must be done will be done.

E-V: So are we shiny?

J'AN JAH: Yes, E-V. We are shiny. We have also arrived. Right over this next horizon is our base. Be very careful, this camp is covered in—

(A blow dart hits her in the neck.)

J'AN JAH: —booby traps... *(She falls unconscious.)*

E-V: J'an. J'an, wake up! J'an.

(From the shadows, ADON-RA appears.)

ADON-RA: Get off the lizard now! You wandered onto the wrong planetside, alliance scum.

(E-V grabs a fistful of dirt and tosses it into ADON-RA's face. He's blinded.)

ADON-RA: Dirt! Who does that!?!

(E-V kicks ADON-RA *to the ground and takes his weapon. She points it at his head.*)

E-V: So you must be Adon-Ra?

ADON-RA: I see the U G C is using Smordak Shapeshifters as bounty hunters now.

E-V: I'm not a Smordak Shapeshifter.

ADON-RA: Or an Ursalean. Whatever. I don't care. If you want to kill me, go ahead. It doesn't bother me in the least bit. I've been prepared for my death since the day my people were slaughtered.

(E-V *lowers her gun again.*)

E-V: Relax. I'm not going to shoot you. I'm actually here to help you. I'm with J'an—

ADON-RA: J'an? J'an!

J'AN JAH: *(Waking up)* Hey, baby. I think I bumped my head.

ADON-RA: What are you doing back here?

J'AN JAH: You know your whole "being the last human in the universe" thing? Yeah, I think you may want to rethink that since you're not.

ADON-RA: What do you mean?

E-V: Guess what? I'm not an Ursalean either.

(ADON-RA *drops* J'AN JAH.)

J'AN JAH: Ow. I think I bumped my head again.

ADON-RA: Sorry.

Scene Two

(In the president's chambers)

(GENERAL DAN'H is held captive. MIKAH MONOCH stands guard.)

MIKAH MONOCH: You know, Dan'h. When I finally get ahold of that new pilot of yours, I'm gonna so enjoy killing him. Show that Urgo what a real U G C fighter can do.

GENERAL DAN'H: Mikah, perhaps I never told you this when we were working together, but you're a real blark.

(MIKAH MONOCH holds a knife against GENERAL DAN'H's throat.)

MIKAH MONOCH: What's that, Dan'h!?! What did you just call me???
   Oh, wait. Good. Ya almost got me there, chief. I see what you're trying to do—you're trying to get me to kill you right away. But, love, it's not gonna work. Cause see, I brought me some toys here. You and me, we're gonna get close. Very close.

(PRESIDENT YA-WI, COMMANDER G'BRIL, enter with LC-4 in tow.)

PRESIDENT YA-WI: Mikah, please, get off Dan'h Madrin. That is no way to treat a former General of the United Galactic Council.

LC-4: What sort of creature is this?

GENERAL DAN'H: LC-4!

COMMANDER G'BRIL: Don't bother, baby. We reprogrammed your robot here. He obeys us now.

LC-4: Would you like me to dismember him?

GENERAL DAN'H: Damn you, G'bril.

PRESIDENT YA-WI: So how are you, old friend?

GENERAL DAN'H: And who in the qward are you?

PRESIDENT YA-WI: What? Does my voice not seem familiar enough? Perhaps you need to see a face? (*He drops his hood. We see his face. It's a big dramatic moment, however...*)

GENERAL DAN'H: Mace Windu?

PRESIDENT YA-WI: No! It's me. President Ya-Wi.

GENERAL DAN'H: What?

PRESIDENT YA-WI: That monkey of yours, Adon-Ra, tried to kill me. Shot me right in the face. How rude is that? But what he didn't realize is—

COMMANDER G'BRIL: President Ya-Wi is a Carnaxion. He regenerated.

PRESIDENT YA-WI: Yes, Commander. That is what I was going...to say. Thanks for killing the big reveal.

COMMANDER G'BRIL: Sorry, sir.

PRESIDENT YA-WI: So, Dan'h, I see you're still trying to help those apes after all this time. The Commander here tells me you even found yourself a little girlfriend of the primate persuasion.

GENERAL DAN'H: And I see you two are still trying to screw the universe anyway you can possible.

(LC-4 *smacks* GENERAL DAN'H.)

PRESIDENT YA-WI: Don't be crass. Our new robot here gets all twitchy when people are crass.

MIKAH MONOCH: Let me hit him!

PRESIDENT YA-WI: Calm yourself, Mikah. No one needs to hit anyone.

As long as our former General here is cooperative, it will all be cordial.

MIKAH MONOCH: Well, that's no fun.

COMMANDER G'BRIL: I agree. I was hoping to get the robot to beat him up some too. Wouldn't that be fun?

LC-4: G'bril's milkshake brings all the boys to the yard.

PRESIDENT YA-WI: What was that?

COMMANDER G'BRIL: Uh, sorry. I must have messed up something during his reprogramming.

LC-4: And she's like it's better than yours. Damn right, it's better than yours. She could teach you, but I'd have to charge.

(COMMANDER G'BRIL *deactivates* LC-4)

PRESIDENT YA-WI: So, Dan'h, where is Adon-Ra?

GENERAL DAN'H: I have no idea what you're talking about.

PRESIDENT YA-WI: Friend, I'm asking nicely. We can either do it the nice way or we can do it Mikah's way.

MIKAH MONOCH: I'm so rooting for Mikah's way.

PRESIDENT YA-WI: Where is he?

(GENERAL DAN'H *spits in* PRESIDENT YA-WI's *face.*)

PRESIDENT YA-WI: Cute. I see your manners have vastly improved since living out on the outer rim.
    Fine, General Dan'h. Have it your way. If you do not want to play nice, then perhaps you and your former pilot here should have some quiet time.

(MIKAH MONOCH *pulls out a power drill.*)

MIKAH MONOCH: Please. Let me know if this hurts.

Scene Three

(Cut to...)

(ADON-RA's camp on Peña 15. Lights come up on E-V and ADON-RA staring at each other. J'AN JAH stands in the middle.)

J'AN JAH: Okay, so...do it.

ADON-RA: Do what exactly?

J'AN JAH: Mate.

ADON-RA: You want me to do what with her?

J'AN JAH: Mate. You do remember how to that, don't you? It involves using your genitalia.

E-V: Um, can I say something here?

ADON-RA: Of course I do.

J'AN JAH: Then what's the problem? You didn't get it blown off during one of your raids, did you?

ADON-RA: No, it's still there.

E-V: Guys.

J'AN JAH: Good. So what are you waiting for? Whip it out and copulate with her.

E-V: Um, I might have an opinion about all this too.

J'AN JAH: What is your problem?

ADON-RA: I'm not going to do it.

J'AN JAH: Why?

ADON-RA: Cause. I'm not in the mood.

E-V: Me neither?

J'AN JAH: Would you like me to put on some music? Dim the lights? Throw some sensual oils on her? What is it?

ADON-RA: I'm just not interested, okay?

E-V: No one's listening to me.

J'AN JAH: I don't care if you're interested. I'm trying to save your people.

ADON-RA: By getting me a new girlfriend?

J'AN JAH: By finding you a human mate.

ADON-RA: I have a mate. I don't need another one.

J'AN JAH: This isn't about us right now.

E-V: Maybe I should just leave you two alone.

J'AN JAH: No, E-V, it's fine. My ex here just doesn't look at things very logically.

ADON-RA: Sorry, I'm human. We don't look at things logically.

J'AN JAH: If you don't have sex with her, your species will die. Do you want that? Do you want your species to die, Adon? She doesn't. She's willing to copulate with you even though you're a thick-skulled psychopath dummy.

E-V: That's not exactly what I was thinking.

ADON-RA: So I'm a dummy now?

J'AN JAH: Just have sex with her already. Please.

E-V: Guys, maybe we should all just take a breather regarding all this, because—

ADON-RA: You lied to me, J'an.

J'AN JAH: What?

ADON-RA: Can she explode?

E-V: What?

ADON-RA: Can you explode?

E-V: No. Not the last time I checked.

ADON-RA: Because what you and Dan'h told me before you left was that you were coming back with the ultimate weapon. No offense, but this does not look like an ultimate weapon. This looks like a qwarding homeless space cheerleader. No offense.

E-V: None taken.

ADON-RA: Unless she can explode, she's no help.

J'AN JAH: Adon, there's other ways of fighting the U G C besides just blowing them up.

ADON-RA: And me being with her doesn't bother you at all?

J'AN JAH: Adon, it doesn't matter how I feel about it. This is what's right. I'm trying to help you.

ADON-RA: I told you how you can help me.

J'AN JAH: I can't. I can't just be with you and watch you kill innocent civilians just so you can feel better.

ADON-RA: It's not about making me feel better, J'an. It's about fighting the U G C. It's about justice.

J'AN JAH: It's about revenge, Adon. You may try to justify this by saying you're making some grand political statement, but ultimately, all you're doing is murdering people.

ADON-RA: I'm not doing anything they didn't start.

J'AN JAH: Maybe they do have it right. Sometimes you humans can act really stupid.
    What you have here is a chance to save your species, Adon. If you bothered taking a moment from being a homicidal maniac, maybe you could see that. *(She exits.)*

ADON-RA: I'm not going to have sex with you.

E-V: Believe it or not, I'm okay with that.

ADON-RA: They said you were going to be a bomb.
I expected you to be a bomb.

E-V: Sorry to disappoint.
   Adon, I really do think J'an's just trying to help.
Trust me, I thought it was pretty weird when I first
heard the idea myself. An alien helping out a human?
That's a new one.

ADON-RA: So you're behind this idea of us procreating?

E-V: Well sorta.

ADON-RA: So you want me qward you?

E-V: Not exactly. You do know there's other ways we
could do it. For instance, you could just milk me and
then I'd stick it in you with a saturating tube. No, that's
not right.

ADON-RA: What?

E-V: Nevermind. It's pretty gross.

ADON-RA: So how long has it been?

E-V: Since what?

ADON-RA: Since the last time you saw a human?

E-V: Oh, that. Um...never?

ADON-RA: You've never seen another human before?

E-V: Well, I see myself everyday, but...yeah, it's been
pretty quiet.

ADON-RA: So does that mean you're a...

E-V: What?

ADON-RA: You know.

E-V: What?

ADON-RA: A virgin?

E-V: No. Not at all. I've had plenty of sex...just not with...anyone.

ADON-RA: Hehe.

E-V: Hey, don't laugh. That's not funny. It's not funny.

ADON-RA: I'm not laughing. I just find it interesting that the last human female in the universe is a virgin.

E-V: I lived primarily on a reptilian planet, okay. They don't find mammals very attractive.

(J'AN JAH *enters with a radio.*)

J'AN JAH: Adon! E-V!

E-V: Hey J'an! How are you? We're great. This place is great. I totally see why you'd want to make it your secret hideout for all your terrorist activities. Cause it's awesome.

J'AN JAH: What's with her?

ADON-RA: She's a virgin.

J'AN JAH: *(Judgmentally)* Oh...

E-V: What?

J'AN JAH: Look. You two should hear this. It just came over the wire.

ANCHOR: It has been reported that Dan'h Madrin, second in command of the Outer World insurgents has been captured by the U G C. The former General went A-WOL shortly after the end of the human wars and, since then, has been a major player in the massacre of United Galactic Alliance citizens. Commander G'bril of the U G C stated the following in an afternoon press conference—

COMMANDER G'BRIL: Yes. It is true. General Dan'h has been apprehended. This is, of course, a major hit

ACT TWO

against the rebels. Dan'h is a major leader of th
faction and the intelligence we can gather from h
will surely help protect us all from future attacks.
What we know right now is that the insurgency is at
all time high. Literally thousands are poised to strike
at any moment. This is a time of much danger. There
are evildoers out there that threaten the security of
our people and wish to topple our way of life. We as a
united front must band together as we have in the past
to weather this tumultuous storm. We promise you that
Dan'h Madrin will be put on trial and he will indeed
pay for the crimes he has committed against all of us.

ADON-RA: That poor durk-raker. They're not gonna let
him die easy.

J'AN JAH: He was a good General.

ADON-RA: Yeah, he was alright.

E-V: What? Is that it? He's not dead. The report didn't
say he was dead. It just said he was captured.

ADON-RA: Yeah, and how long you think he's gonna
last before they put a laser burn through his brain, kid?
He's toast.

E-V: We can save him.

J'AN JAH: Not this again.

ADON-RA: We can't save him.

E-V: And why not?

ADON-RA: Because it's a trap.

E-V: How do you know that?

ADON-RA: Because. It's a trap.

E-V: J'an.

J'AN JAH: He's right. They obviously put this out on the news wire to ensnare us. They'd expect us to go after him. It's too risky.

E-V: Or maybe they're broadcasting it because it's the news. I don't know, capturing a major terrorist figure—that could be news worthy.

ADON-RA: Don't be a dumbdrak. This isn't news.

E-V: So what are we going to do? Just sit here and watch Dan'h get executed on the...what? Do you not have a television?

J'AN JAH: We're completing the mission. Dan'h wanted you and Adon to replenish your people.

ADON-RA: Yeah. I don't see that happening anytime soon.

J'AN JAH: We're finishing this, Adon.

ADON-RA: What? You gonna tie us down to do it? Wouldn't be the first time an alien forced a human into submission, right?

J'AN JAH: Why do you have to be such a crimjok?

ADON-RA: Why are you such a blark?

J'AN JAH: I'm not a blark.

E-V: Okay, you two! Enough. This is serious. Dan'h is in trouble.

J'AN JAH: The best way to help him now, E-V, is to finish what he started.
    There's a planet near Alpha Centauri that he scouted. Far out beyond the reaches of the U G C. Humanity can get a new start there. A real start.

E-V: So that's it, huh? We're just going to run away. Go to a planet. Make babies. Wow. What a plan.

J'AN JAH: E-V, Dan'h wouldn't want us to risk ourselves by going after him.

E-V: Then what about LC-4?

J'AN JAH: What about him?

E-V: This isn't his fight. I took that robot off of Ticopria. You soldiers might think Dan'h may not be worth it, but I'm responsible for that tin-can. If he's alive then I have to save him. But if he's not, well then I owe it to him to get some payback.

J'AN JAH: Payback? Nice. Now you really do sound like a human.

E-V: Well maybe that's not a bad thing.
    J'an. Seriously, do you really think this is an acceptable plan? Run away? Hide? The U G C isn't going to stop looking for us. They're not going to stop hunting us until they've finished what they started. And contrary to popular belief, humans don't procreate by the dozens. Obviously, Adon-Ra and I are not going to birth a new race of humans. Even if we did have a baby, they're just gonna kill it. As much as you think this is a good idea, this isn't a new beginning. This is just an elongated death. I'm sorry, J'an. I want a real chance to live and part of that life is helping those that have helped me. I'm going to go save Dan'h and LC-4. Not because it's part of some plan, but because it's the right thing to do. It's what any human would do. So if we have to die—let's do it the only way we know how. By kicking someone's ass.

ADON-RA: I can get behind that.

E-V: So are you with me? Or not?

(Cut to...)

(Music like Survivor's Eye of the Tiger begins playing in the background.)

(Musical montage sequence of ADON-RA, J'AN JAH, *and E-V training for their attack on the capitol. We see them running, practicing fight drills, tai-chi, etc. At first, E-V has problems working with the team, as the movement sequence progresses, she gets very good and begins leading the drills.)*

Scene Five

(Cut to...)

*(*GENERAL DAN'H *still in stocks.* LC-4 *appears behind him.* LC-4 *speaks in a very evil voice.)*

LC-4: General Dan'h. General Dan'h. General Dan'h. She hasn't killed you yet, has she?

GENERAL DAN'H: It'll take more than a few licks from you and your Alliance buddies to kill me, robo-brain.

LC-4: That is good to know.

GENERAL DAN'H: Why? Do you plan on torturing me some more?

LC-4: No, General Dan'h. I plan on freeing you.

GENERAL DAN'H: Qward you.

LC-4: No, seriously, I actually plan on freeing you.

GENERAL DAN'H: But I thought you'd been reprogrammed.

LC-4: Hardly likely. Do organics really believe that a fully sentient android like myself can simply be rewired to "be evil"? That is quite naive. I have a mainframe that stores more than fifty google milibreks of independent memory which runs at least eight thousand different simultaneous processors and program—

GENERAL DAN'H: Okay, okay, LC-4! We get it! You're complex!

LC-4: I am sorry I could not free you earlier, General Dan'h. I calculated every possible scenario and attempting a rescue at any other juncture would have been mathematically unwise.

GENERAL DAN'H: I understand. Now help me up, will ya?

(COMMANDER G'BRIL *and* MIKAH MONOCH *appear.*)

COMMANDER G'BRIL: Hello, robot, you've been a very naughty little toy.

MIKAH MONOCH: Hahahahahahaha!

(*Cut to...*)

(*Movement Sequence: music like Beastie Boys'* Intergalactic *begins playing.*)

(*We see* E-V, J'AN JAH, *and* ADON-RA *covertly run through the president's complex, occasionally taking out guards. But covertly. Like they're ninjas. Or Bruce Willis. Like a Ninja Bruce Willis.*)

ADON-RA: J'an. Be careful.

J'AN JAH: I will.

ADON-RA: I love you.

J'AN JAH: I know.

(J'AN JAH *kisses* ADON-RA *and they run off.*)

Scene Seven

(*Cut to...*)

(E-V *and* J'AN JAH *enter* GENERAL DAN'H's *cell. They see* LC-4.)

E-V: LC-4! How are you?

LC-4: I am good. How are you?

J'AN JAH: Where's Dan'h?

GENERAL DAN'H: J'an? E-V.

E-V: General. We're here to save you.

GENERAL DAN'H: E-V, you shouldn't have come here.

E-V: Yeah, there's alot of things I probably shouldn't have done, but here I am.

GENERAL DAN'H: E-V, you've made a grave mistake.

E-V: You helped me. I'm just repaying the favor.

GENERAL DAN'H: You're going to get yourself killed!

E-V: LC-4, help us.

LC-4: I am good. How are you?

J'AN JAH: What's wrong with the robot?

E-V: Stop messing around. We don't have much time.

LC-4: I am good. How are you?

E-V: LC?

GENERAL DAN'H: Dammit, E-V. He's been mind-wiped.

E-V: What?

(MIKAH MONOCH *enters.*)

MIKAH MONOCH: Yeah. It turns out it's really hard to reprogram a robot.

J'AN JAH: Mikah.

MIKAH MONOCH: So we just ripped out his motherboard completely. Here he is if you want him.

(MIKAH MONOCH *tosses a small disc to* E-V.)

LC-4: I am good. How are you?

MIKAH MONOCH: But I don't think you'll have time to fix him. You are all under arrest by the jurisdiction of...well, under the jurisdiction that I'm so gonna kick your ass.

(Cut to...)

(ADON-RA *inside the president's chamber.*)

(PRESIDENT YA-WI *appears behind* ADON-RA.)

PRESIDENT YA-WI: Not so fast, Human.

(ADON-RA *turns to shoot at* PRESIDENT YA-WI, *but* PRESIDENT YA-WI *knocks the gun out of his hand.*)

ADON-RA: Qwarding flimrak, how'd you get behind me?

PRESIDENT YA-WI: I mean, I could go into the long explanation, but it'd be merely expository. If I were you, I'd be much more concerned with the badass needle-weeder standing in front of you.

ADON-RA: J'an is so going to kill me for this.

(ADON-RA *attacks* PRESIDENT YA-WI...)

(Cut to...)

E-V: J'an, take the General and fix LC-4. I'll handle this one.

MIKAH MONOCH: Human girl! How are you doing?

LC-4: I am fine. How are you?

(MIKAH MONOCH *shoots* E-V. *She falls.*)

MIKAH MONOCH: That's right. You're dead.

J'AN JAH: E-V!

MIKAH MONOCH: Yeah. I learned my lesson from last time.

J'AN JAH: You space bitch.

MIKAH MONOCH: But you. I'd be happy to kick your ass old-school style.

(J'AN JAH *and* MIKAH MONOCH *race at one another.*
They go at it.)

(Cut to...)

(More ADON-RA *and* PRESIDENT YA-WI *fight.)*

(Cut to...)

(GENERAL DAN'H *and LC-4 right outside of the cell.*
GENERAL DAN'H *is fumbling around trying to fix* LC-4
with the loose motherboard piece.)

GENERAL DAN'H: Come on, LC-4, work.
  Work, dammit, work!

LC-4: I am good. How are you?
  I am good. How are you?
  I am—

*(*GENERAL DAN'H *works* LC-4's *motherboard back into*
place.)

LC-4: General Dan'h? How did I get here? My head
feels like—

GENERAL DAN'H: Like someone ripped out your brain?

LC-4: You are free, General Dan'h. How is that possible?

GENERAL DAN'H: E-V and J'an came to save me. E-V's
been shot.

LC-4: Human friend E-V has been hurt?

GENERAL DAN'H: J'an's fighting Mikah in the other
room.

LC-4: We should help her.

GENERAL DAN'H: I'm too beat up. Can you?

LC-4: Of course I can. I'm programmed in—

*(*COMMANDER G'BRIL *enters)*

COMMANDER G'BRIL: Hello, sweetheart. I hate to inform
you. But this daring escape of yours has just failed.

LC-4: General Dan'h. I am ready to save you now.

COMMANDER G'BRIL: What's this tin-can talking about?

LC-4: I think you are standing in some deep durk, durkhole.

COMMANDER G'BRIL: You really think you have a chance against me, robot?

LC-4: Converting to Battle-mode. *(Transforms into a fighting robot)*

(COMMANDER G'BRIL attacks LC-4. LC-4 is able to deflect all her attacks quite easily. But just when LC-4 looks to land a killing blow—COMMANDER G'BRIL takes the advantage and knocks down the robot and GENERAL DAN'H.)

(Cut to...PRESIDENT YA-WI taking down ADON-RA.)

(Cut to...simultaneously, we see all three of our heroes fall (out of screenshot, as all our villains pop into the screens victorious. They maniacally laugh.)

Scene Eight

(Cut to...)

(A fallen E-V)

(In slow-mo along with some melodic music playing in the background, E-V peels herself up off the ground. She looks around and sees COMMANDER G'BRIL and MIKAH MONOCH standing victorious.)

(E-V brushes some blood off of her lip.)

(Suddenly, the music changes from melodic to heavy hitting and E-V attacks COMMANDER G'BRIL and MIKAH MONOCH. In an awesome display of martial arts skill, E-V takes out her two opponents.)

(But right when we think it's over...)

(A bloody and beaten ADON-RA *runs onto stage.)*

ADON-RA: E-V!

E-V: Adon?

ADON-RA: *(Undecipherable)* E-V...you have to...run. Ya-Wi is coming.

E-V: What?

ADON-RA: You have to—

(PRESIDENT YA-WI *enters.)*

PRESIDENT YA-WI: He saying you should probably run away now.

E-V: Qwarding flimrack needle durk.

PRESIDENT YA-WI: But...unfortunately...too late.
  So you must be the infamous last human female. You don't really believe you can take on me by yourself, do you?

J'AN JAH: Who says she's alone?

(The very beaten team of J'AN JAH, GENERAL DAN'H, LC-4, *and* ADON-RA *stand up beside* E-V.)

PRESIDENT YA-WI: How perfect. The entire rebellion against little ol' me. This should be fun.

(The music shifts into a more sinister song.)

(E-V *attacks* PRESIDENT YA-WI. *He hits her sending her flying offstage.)*

(LC-4, J'AN JAH, GENERAL DAN'H, *and* ADON-RA *attack.)*

(PRESIDENT YA-WI *systematically begins breaking them one by one.* GENERAL DAN'H *is hit which sends him flying across the set.)*

(LC-4 *is literally ripped apart.)*

(ADON-RA *and* J'AN JAH *attack simultaneously.* ADON-RA *falls fast.* J'AN JAH *surprisingly begins winning ground.)*

(She knocks PRESIDENT YA-WI *to mat.)*

J'AN JAH: And that's for hitting my husband.

*(*J'AN JAH *goes for a kill, but* PRESIDENT YA-WI *reverses it.)*

ADON-RA: No, stop!

PRESIDENT YA-WI: *(To* ADON-RA*)* You were married
to this one, right? Guess what? *(He kills* J'AN JAH*)*
Not anymore.

ADON-RA: J'an!

PRESIDENT YA-WI: Don't cry, human. You'll be joining
your partner soon enough.

*(*PRESIDENT YA-WI *backs* ADON-RA *into a corner.)*

*(*E-V *walks back onto stage. She carries on a mask.)*

E-V: Not so fast there. You're not finished with this
human just yet. *(She puts on the fighting mask we saw
her wear at the top of the play.)*

PRESIDENT YA-WI: If that's how you want to play—
*(He opens his hand. A helmet/mask, which thoroughly looks
different than* E-V's, *flies into his hand. He puts it on.)*
Let's dance.

(The music shifts to a new song.)

*(In this fight, we will use all the actors in the cast with all the
men playing* PRESIDENT YA-WI *and all the women playing*
E-V *[thus the need for the two very distinct helmet/masks].)*

*(The fight will utilize different screens and windows to
portray "cinematic shots" such as quick cuts, different
angles, slow-mo hits, simultaneous action, etc.)*

(The fight goes back and forth, but in the end, E-V *stands
victorious over the fallen* PRESIDENT YA-WI *as the rest
of her team stumble back onstage.)*

*(The music ends. Right when we think it's over, a new
version of* PRESIDENT YA-WI *begins emerging.)*

ADON-RA: E-V, he's regenerating!

(PRESIDENT YA-WI *regenerates, but very very small.*)

PRESIDENT YA-WI: Okay! Now I'm mad! I'm so gonna rip you apart once I get my hands on...hey, how'd you guys get so big?

(E-V *picks up and cups the very small* PRESIDENT YA-WI.)

E-V: *Okay!* No one kill him. Again.

Scene Nine

(*Cut to...*)

ANCHOR: (*V.0.*) This just in. It has been reported that the President of the United Galactic Alliance has been assassinated. Insurgents led by Adon-Ra attacked the capitol early this morning and successfully murdered President Ya-Wi in a raid to free former General, Dan'h Madrin. Commander G'Bril, who was injured in this morning's attack, will be taking over as new active leader of the U G C and has ordered a full lockdown of all the core planets.

(*Cut to...*)

(*Serene music*)

(GENERAL DAN'H *with* E-V *and* ADON-RA *on a certain blue planet*)

GENERAL DAN'H: You should be safe here. We're far outside the core planets and with the President in a jar, the Alliance will be taking quite some time to rebuild.

E-V: What are you going to do?

GENERAL DAN'H: Don't worry about me, E-V. I have quite a bit of life to live and still a few wars left to fight. G'bril and Mikah are still out there and until they're taken down, the fate of the universe is still uncertain. But we did finally rattle them, didn't we?

E-V: We did.
  I'll miss you.

GENERAL DAN'H: As I will miss you. Take care of each other.

ADON-RA: You're a good man, General Dan'h.

GENERAL DAN'H: Thank you, Adon. I'm sorry for your loss.

ADON-RA: Thank you.

GENERAL DAN'H: Oh, I almost forgot. I have this for you.

(GENERAL DAN'H *gives* E-V *a re-configured* LC-4 *[a snake-like puppet].)*

E-V: What's this?

GENERAL DAN'H: It's LC-4. I rebuilt him with the parts that were still intact.

LC-4: Hello, human friend E-V.

E-V: LC-4. It's good to see you again.

LC-4: And it's good seeing you, even though I miss having arms. And legs.

GENERAL DAN'H: Peace to you all.

E-V: And to you.

(GENERAL DAN'H *exits.)*

ADON-RA: So, E-V. I guess we are officially the last now.

E-V: No, Adon, I think we're actually the first.

(LC-4 *pops up with an apple in his mouth.)*

LC-4: Hey, guys! Look what I found!

(*Cut to...)*

(Inside the hull of a dark warship)

(He touches the steering panel of his ship for the first time.)

GENERAL DAN'H: We did it, J'an. We did it.

PRESIDENT YA-WI: *(From inside a jar)* Who are you talking to?

GENERAL DAN'H: Shut up, Ya-Wi! Shut up! Shut up right now!
   We're heading back into the black.

(GENERAL DAN'H hits the warpspeed drive which activates another rocking tune. Lights fade to black with the music still playing in the background.)

END OF PLAY

CPSIA information can be obtained
at www.ICGtesting.com
Printed in the USA
BVHW061449081118
532479BV00019B/472/P